RYAN KNIGHTON

Swing in the Hollow

(poems)

ANVIL PRESS • VANCOUVER

Swing in the Hollow

Copyright © 2001 by Ryan Knighton

All rights reserved. No part of this book may be reproduced by any means without the prior written permission of the publisher, with the exception of brief passages in reviews. Any request for photocopying or other reprographic copying of any part of this book must be directed in writing to the Canadian Copyright Licensing Agency (CANCOPY) One Yonge Street, Suite 1900, Toronto, Ontario, Canada, M5E 1E5.

Printed and bound in Canada
Cover design: Rayola Graphic Design
Author photo: Tracy Rawa
Cover Photos: Robert Sherrin

CANADIAN CATALOGUING IN PUBLICATION DATA

Knighton, Ryan

   Swing in the hollow

   Poems.
   ISBN 1-895636-34-5

I. Title
PS8571.N55S9 2001   C811'.6   C00-911576-5
PR9199.3.K54S9 2001

Represented in Canada by the Literary Press Group
Distributed by General Distribution Services

The publisher gratefully acknowledges the financial assistance of the B.C. Arts Council, the Canada Council for the Arts, and the Book Publishing Industry Development Program (BPIDP) for their support of our publishing program.

Anvil Press
Suite 204-A 175 East Broadway,
Vancouver, B.C. V5T 1W2 CANADA
www.anvilpress.com

TABLE OF CONTENTS

WHAT LEAVES US
So What / 9
Braille / 10
Moving Sonnet / 11
A Comfort of Metaphors / 12
Method / 14
Spells Galileo / 15
Night in the Riverbed / 17
Mr. Universe / 18
Species / 19
Poem from a Pumpkin / 20
Crawlspace / 21
Redeeming the Portuguese Club / 22
The Ideal Grandmother / 24
Music Note / 26
Insomnia / 27
Charlie Don't Surf / 28
Lamp / 29
If in the Same River / 30
What Leaves Us / 33
Antipoetry / 34

FROM CHARLES STREET, PANDEMONIUM
"In Milton's plot, his paradise" / 37
"As if they've come to the end" / 40
"His daughters read" / 41
"What you saw first & couldn't" / 43
"I live in a neighbourhood" / 44
"Babysat parkside by the old" / 45
"What's her name, John" / 47
"After the nosey habit-" / 49
"Spring? It happens" / 50
"Some of the faceless" / 52
"In the heart of the plot, John" / 54
"The blue TV" / 57
"Before he backed" / 60
"Back on the bleached" / 62

COLOUR THEORY

Emergency Broadcast System / 67
Mr. Universe, the First / 68
A Comfort of Metaphors: Summer Reading / 69
The Ballad of Echolocation / 70
Blues for Dashboard Mary / 72
Henri Bergson Gone Done / 74
Visa / 76
Anitpoetry, Animorph / 77
Teenage Preludes / 78
When the Yard Sale Bought It / 80
Method (II) / 82
Five Deep Cove Stanzas / 83
What Leaves Us: Seasonal Hymn / 84
On About / 85
Gluttony / 87
Cutting the National Tracks: A Purdy / 88
Graven Image Tag / 92
The Wickedness That Sleeps in Stone / 95
'brother of death and forgetting . . .' / 97
Colour Theory / 99

Acknowledgements

for my parents, Miles & Kathie
for Tracy, of course

& in memory of my brother
Rory Patrick Knighton / 1977-99

> He wants to be
> a brutal old man,
> an aggressive old man,
> as dull, as brutal
> as the emptiness around him.
> —*Robert Creeley*

WHAT LEAVES US

a temporary language

as temporary things

and poetry the

math

—Larry Eigner

So What

Once did I happen
to catch Miles Davis
at the corner grocer's.

Not at a loss
really lost
for directions
finding his way
over the PA
but unusual
in a routine
of aisles

& holding an Orange Crush
to his open ear
so cool there
alone in front
of the cooler.

I buy cigarettes over
& over the counter
again "Smoking
Can Kill You" never

"Reduces Life Expectancy"
as if expected.
Miles slips out (did he
pay?) filling his mouth

with the sound of oranges.
I'm no original

lay down the 5 bucks.
From my pocket
draw my only
crumpled bluenote.

BRAILLE

It is January goosebumps, is noon-hour sand
in your sandals & sometimes when you're four
it's bare feet clutching barnacles
in Pender Harbour. That same year
it's your father's whiskers on your cheek
& a July heat rash in your palms, it is gravel
at 16 under balding tires & it is an eternity
of ha ha ha ha after midnight.

Once it's an itchiness from the neighbour's lawn
& maybe that summer it is pavement
under your chin—it is definitely the stitches
that followed & my recently shaved head.
It is never rubbing a fish
the wrong way & is in the spider's legs
you were afraid to touch. It is a late supper
of brown rice & asparagus tips on your tongue
& it's any particular set of bedtime fingertips.
Vancouver's light Autumn drizzle is what it is
& it's finally pressing stars to dial God.

Moving Sonnet
for Jack Spicer

But little of the year's remains are
shaped for a box. Shuffling feet
yellowing carpet & this old space   jumps
with electricity.   Static   bounds
slipper to finger to light   switch.
Anywhere it can reach—a collector's eye at

Sotheby's, like amateur video.   We move
& it moves us.

Casing time till the floor's Chinese tea.
Leaves lint bits of stuff & tape—each
its own orphan   entry
packed in entropy.

Elsewhere someone settles tomorrow
among the impossibility of furniture.

A Comfort of Metaphors

If a dart is only the half of it, in part
its companionship that final

clumsy thud of cork accused by your point
then you say, 'I meant to do that.' Thin laughter.

They fly in a rhetoric of feathers
imparted in syllogisms.

Assume Monte draws Guinness for us
the antennae of his busted pinky
alert. Imagine the Queen

(only battered looking)
taking high tea. She sips
politely pointing to her crown.

& when the muddy uprising settles
down Monte engraves
a lucky clover in every head.

A skill it is to be certain.
Thick with beer at the close

what thoughts we have
of each other. Aimless

nights winning the love
of accidental friends gathered round.

As the conceit takes you
extend your arm as far as it will.

The rules they
make it beautiful, the game

to hit the heart of them all.
When you strike

cheers.
It's the Queen that nags.

Method

under glass
table
sunshine
this pity cat
sleeps
toppled-down tired
Ellie-still

      then
            the Sphinx   purrs
                      hieroglyphics
               away yawns   3000 years
                           maybe
                  stirs Cairo
                        to shed
              a good coat
                    of museum dust
             with her bedlam
      tongue

Spells Galileo

Huffing home from the Community Centre
the closest to us, burning

Sun maps itself
all over the equations
of my shoulders & scalp

My belly yellowing
to proof

Inside the cotton moment
lift off, holy cow it's hot
in the gap

When The Gap unveils its ridiculous
sweatshirtiness

& a self presses
through its Pope Mobile

Would gladly share in
the air taken
in by the mighty Ali
& all his gravity

When he murdered a rock
& he somethinged a brick
& said something else
& made medicine sick

But the workout
it never feels its finish
just this soft expanding
of its laws

So dizzy wheezing
I'm Lone Ranger pasty

hoofing home over mountain & mesa
Silver dead over yonder
gone to the great glue factory

& we're sorry he is
the poor goner

Night in the Riverbed

Pulled by the green chain
of hours, another day of dying
grey light scaled & fell
from the coast. Someone saw
its secret quicksilver
water carved to flesh.

Here you submerge
under quilt & air
worrying the pillow
breathing in a collapsed
cotton lung

hooked & drawn
to its soft animal.

Ear pressed to the plaster
it thrashes for more covers
& demands affection

as if you'd throw your tender arm
over all that black fur

its tooth of moon
tugging your bones
your slightest quiver
pawed by a cold grey
eye full of fish.

Mr. Universe

The private balance of weight.
In his dumb hand five & ten pounds.

Taken from the long work.
Out bench raising tablets from mountain bedrock.

Healthy hearty people struck him shallow.
Their gimme shine while he smoked.

& fumed about betrayal like Pan handled.
& Hook he learned how the body pushes.

Its likeness. A good hard look.
In an empty palm its ready parentheses.

How to carry a voice in cupped hands.
For those who would pump it up.

Have a nice day history.
Treasure & bones blasted from the long work.

Out bench your heavy duty.
Future measures up.

He learned to curl each time in a bow.
To his old half-heartedness in the Jazzercise mirror.

How innocent & heartless a figure.
There crunching up on the mat.

A boy buried long in a heavy heavy chest.

SPECIES

To this class of students
English is the job.

It travels heavily about
the room sleepy with latin suffixes.

Today is Dinosaurs, Unit 9,
& past tense comes impossibly,

lumbers across millennia
& continents to be reconstructed

with all the precision
of Friday labour.

& who would give a shit
if it's only to petrify?

& who can finally answer
why they were all dying

to speak.

Poem from a Pumpkin

Waiting in a closet café marking essays
about Dickinson & how much she seems to love Death
or at least his civility. There should be so much more than
what's said. My squiggles & notes
are hiccups when they should be perverse
tattoos & Dickinson should moan through typefaces
Across the street is a pumpkin
stand erected in honour of the harvest season.
I've never noticed orange so much,
so fat & charged.
My father carved one
every year & we watched the blade hungrily
run slow & smooth, willing it to go otherwise
off Magic Marker lines. There should be so much more
than the eyes, nose & mouth—there should be something
other than a lonely head decaying
on the front porch for a week, a euphemism
lit once for witches & one-eyed pirates
not yet itchy to undress the other.
Under sheets at night the ghosts feel
their costumes change & wonder what
they are to be next year.
& there is nothing satisfying or solid
about this red pen or its careful trail
& there should simply be so much more to reveal
with a colour. If I had more than this table setting,
something
larger & sharper than a butter-knife,
I would put Dickinson back in Death's magic
carriage & with the first stroke of midnight carve a nation
of pumpkins, manna spilling floods, secrets oozing through
stilted streets,
& the rushing girth of Fall, embered leaves
& pumpkin guts would open every hole to say
awe.

CRAWLSPACE

We are building caterpillars
from severed egg cartons
green pipe cleaners
drilled through skulls
ready to receive impulses
that are the new world.

My brothers
& perhaps my sister
are crafting the morning
our father phones proclaiming
there is no work.

Down building came
to a crippling halt. Our transformations
seemed wasteful.

Paper products
even the flimsiest
must be more valuable
in original forms.

Redeeming the Portuguese Club

An empty pint glass
tipped by dull light
remembers its edges in white.

Thursday rain runs
Commercial Drive & down
come thirsty regulars

like me. & a jukebox turns
Marvin, Aretha, Ray & Otis.
Names are all I know

bursting through the door,
one jostles another in a chorus
line as if that is history

comin' round. As if we own
the tokens we are about
to receive & for plugging songs

give thanks. What's in hand
is all this turning
to find an image in the light

that holds our light-hearted mugs
together. & meanwhile
keeps calling for one more

round of Motown
to fix the faces
it finds for now.

Sometimes it works, the jukebox,
this light, these glasses
& names. Around here

everyone tips over the page
to pour versions of rain
from the halos of porkpie hats.

The Ideal Grandmother

After being away
sometimes overseas

finding yourself back
you always return
to your grandmother's for supper

She'll phone to tell you
you're back now
it's time to catch up

It's blueberry muffins first
hot iced tea mix & cigarettes
then a steaming plate of Beef Stroganoff

the kind Plato imagines

One time is exceptional
the conversation alive & well
directed

on it's merry way

We might speak of travel
wonder what coastal peoples ate
to avert scurvy
the sailor's scourge

which brings us back to travel

& we might voice our views
on today's politics
how you know a conservative riding
near election time
when the conservatives are in power
by the road quality
in those neighbourhoods

which brings us back to travel

& it's good to be back
& it's good to eat endless meals
& it's good to catch up

& she's glad you raised the subject
as she's been meaning to tell you
for quite some time now
she made a mental note
while you were away
to say
to say

That's how it goes

Music Note

Imagine the girl
collapsing to her seat
descending in scale
that #20 bus musty
in a spittle of rain
muggy in the summer
shining. Her expression.

Borrowed she rocks in its metal
frame carried away
& skittles a party balloon
windy along gravel patches.

Legs unfold to the aisle & she
stretches bony
lyrical lines. Feet carried
in measured leather shoes.

It's a dream I have
dozing a way home waking
downtown startled.

Make the best
mistakes of it all.

A license to fetch
new favourites
from a store of hundreds.
Score some second-
hand tunes this
doggoned day
chasing beauty in transit.

INSOMNIA

Preparing, have a drink & then
another. Winter breeze lifts evening's weight
& the hem of your skirt. These are
the unnecessary theatrics—black cape,
tophat, a rabbit poised, & the trick relaxes
in details.

Being without direction
today lost its mastery. But there is ritual,
a show in the air, purpose piggy-backed
like pollen. Magicians
have a drink & then another,
ready to conjure unrehearsed.
Sleep, a cold run by moonlight.
The wind at your thigh.

On stage there is commitment.
(the dish and spoon running away,
a cow poised . . .)

Later, something raises the sun
& some imagination, grazed
by new light, blooms. Gravity fumbles
through the pillow for leverage
& plucks panic's face. A lonesome moon
elopes. Still you're poised,
you without rabbits.

Charlie Don't Surf

If for no other reason than
Chinese New Year superstition.
Who'd ride the ocean's worried
crest for ten days & risk all that
bad luck? Charlie Don't Surf is an empty sea-
food restaurant, these waters too
calm, ocean tight
in its black leather sleeve.

But more like dance lessons. Shy,
water greets sand & retreats,
leaves tender footprints on the beach's
back for a new year to rehearse,
a pulse of pebbles
waltzing, our feet, one two
three, one two three, it comes
& goes in us.

A few ballroom strangers
along the boardwalk drift,
keep from stumbling
& all that bad luck. A lift

of fingers around my elbow,
their tender squeeze, one two three,
one two three pulsing

a hand that is

a heart that is

a wave

hello.

Lamp

Not sharp against skin
burrowing in or even hewn from
the idea of dawn, this industrious finger
with its cold touch decrees
the invention of darkness
after light.

Flick of first there was.

But off the lamp composes
a specter dying
in the vault of your eye.
This afterlife of things
the briefest of wishes
to ease through your mottled room.

Before these coals
remembering chair & desk
ember & ash, wish you might
but the edge of things continues
to bump you in the night.

Death lights the world
behind its oily palm
pressed to your face.
& for those thousands
or one night to come
here's the rub.

If in the Same River

Sometimes

a glass

of water, sometimes

whiskey.

■ ■ ■

Around the round
tables balance the young

& old who taste beer & talk
nightly.

The old order
another pitcher

drive a fast line
down the field.

Scrambling the young
order

admittedly drunk
but eager to catch

up
with the pitcher.

■ ■ ■

Sometimes
a whiskey

watered back.

◼ ◼ ◼

The young listen
to the music
bar moving to
Ella Fitzgerald.
Smooth sounds
the time
notwithstanding.
The young dream
it is theirs
not jazz but
this drip of memory.
& so gifted
the present
goes on improvising.

◼ ◼ ◼

Sometimes
a drink.

◼ ◼ ◼

Friends turn
up to the music
bar. Joining
in one

finds himself
conflated, it is
Salt Lake City again
1956 falling back
in time
down drunk
in love
all over
us.

How merciful
it is to be there
& here
all over
for instance.

What Leaves Us

Spring, a brittle tissue of maples
still clings to the rotted lawn
with dirty arthritic fingers.
Imagine—Spring—May
asking someone to rake it up
scratch Death's back.

From the bellowed heap
I begin to gather some people
leap to mind

sparks shoot past
consciousness

that porch light
& its frenzy of moths. To me
springs:

> Tracy is eating the olive
> George is raising the umbrella
> Reg is wearing the hat
> Sharon is driving the car

ANTIPOETRY

To know this keep
a pot of eggs on the boil   (keep) (keep)
dawn's desire for a midnight snack
in the a.m. some early form of
pure heartbreak.

12 minutes stimulating eternity.

Whatever happens to be will be
in the fridge & isn't
running for cover. To be finished
with creation & all
it only takes

takes 12 minutes.

Put a lid on it
rumbling water needs turning down
Tracy mumbles. & pull the sky down
a world keeps
keeps running

for cover. Or eat it simply
crack it over the sink
any old egg   (O how many more?)
will run. Tracy can't stand
to rise out from under covers
& reddening her face
the morning sky   (O how deep does it go?)
grows in our kitchen window.
Just another sun glows 12 minutes old it is

running so far. O
the little egg knows
how little keeps
keeps up.

FROM CHARLES STREET, PANDEMONIUM

For Robert Sherrin and his images

■ ■ ■

In Milton's plot, his paradise
inside a darkness
is unearthed by God

realized by Satan no
less. Is unfathomable
to desire to be

flesh bitten by the red
fire that illuminates our lesser world
of loss. It instructs him in waking

to the darkness behind things
greater than us. Before me
like the parts of this rented office

my little room grew all
fragments of shape & sin
from a designer war

we fell into, love
to dwell in Milton's plot.
How many lanterns

did Satan hang
in Pandemonium?
What beauty is best served

by a suspension of small lives
to flicker in the echoing halls?
These chains of irony we hang

brighten the government
of a fierce & fiery place—the cities, Hell
an older smouldering Vancouver.

Sing of these, the beautiful plots that consume
themselves. The bard howled
for Moloch, for the beast's need to burn

but Moloch is the impossibility
of our desire to cease
to be anything but burning.

▣ ▣ ▣

As if they've come to the end
of something serious, the municipal lamps
border Parker St.

crook their wanting necks
looming buzzards
over the fattened body

of this smoky metro-
polis, this brand of leviathan
we pursue

only to move casually inside.
We too have purchased a palace
beside boiling waters. Ashen towers

in a petrified stand
of glazed & longing looks
out to the Pacific.

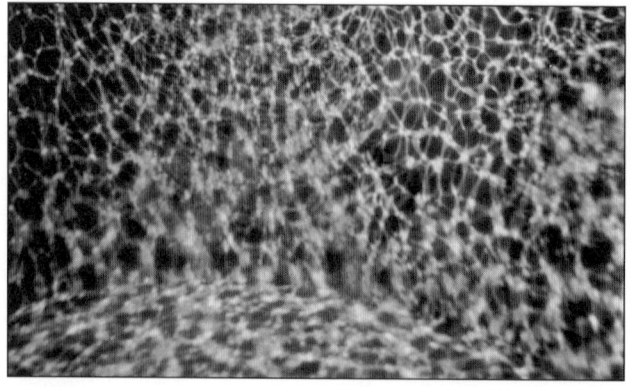

■ ■ ■

His daughters read
& write what he says, what was said
by nobody.

The vision is that
purifying, that searing
it blackened his eyes.

It is not a hard world
to justify, to be touched into
by blindness. I imagine the words

are harder to make
to take this way
their disobedience

as they arrive in dream
with a slap to his head.
But it is her fantastic deliverance

in a soft open hand.
It is a young woman's invocation
of love & resentment I dream of.

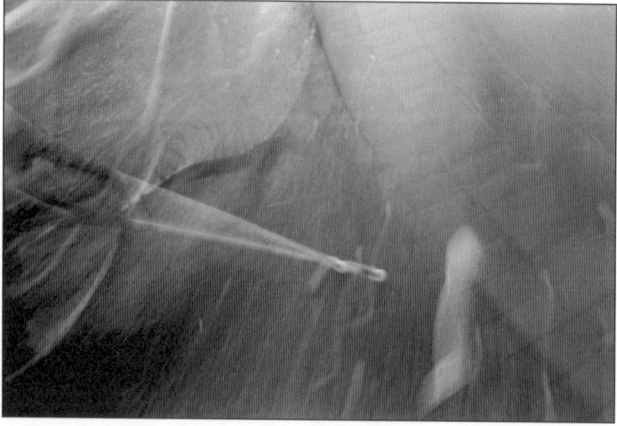

◘ ◘ ◘

What you saw first & couldn't
was a beast (as the story
is told) so large it was like

how large it was like. It
was so much it was not
a beast in need of a name, it

was like the stories of a whale
that was like a mountain
that was like an island

alive like a whale
that is in a sea
if the earth is a stone

in that sea & it is
an island to a whale
or a whale itself. It is the problem

of likeness, see it
swallowed up
in the city's core

the likeness that rises in stories.
Here we live on top
of each other, live

like the evil
of seeming, seeming
epic proportions.

■ ■ ■

I live in a neighbourhood
we called Pandemonium
nurse coffee at small sidewalk tables

& don't smoke inside.
Wild-haired punks & their hounds
hang here

furious on Charles St.
the corner where sidewalk is white
bleached by sun.

They have never been exposed
to an original revolution
& think they want one

or are one, if you can spare
them. Some say they're asking for it
some say change.

Those holding court
who don't smoke inside
freak behind sunglasses

recite city by-laws
hope to disappear the hounds
of Charles St. with words. With hope

others drop coins
in oily hats & beggar baskets
sovereign's head on one side shining.

◼ ◼ ◼

Babysat parkside by the old
ideas, munching gold nuggets
hot from the deep

fryer. Just chicken, that
is me distracted by the old ideas
of old men in a green park.

I mean to learn from
likeness before it passes
to let it

dip sweet
& sourly. Phenomenal
to watch Alexandria

kinda. Cool in the
sleeveless shirts of good
guys, I think I hear

a player shout he's open.
I'm rooting for
other people's desires

to be a people
who trust the hard ball
will fire into

& out of place. Just like that
I'd give my right
eye up

to the wind.
Ignore the old man's holler
on his own run-

down porch, the usual barter
of costs with the contractor
for a few extra bucks

Pascal kicks his rusty gate. The ambling men
ideal in brown trousers circle
the bocce pit twilight.

Please speak up
to me of Dante I ask
them but wouldn't.

■ ■ ■

What's her name, John
the voice that sustains you
in this daring place, in this hour

& its long Spring shadows?
Does she have voice mail?
I've heard she's in Yaletown

between jobs, stuck in a
leaky condo, chased to the edge
of False Creek by committees.

Sometimes I think I can hear her
through the flapping
venetians, delivered

with the rattle of consumption.
I wake, rise, open the blinds & look defiantly
down on my back alley

but it's the Britannia schoolgirls
again & the bewitching fall
of their designer shoes.

Over there's the Sikh temple
back wall protesting "Britannia
Rules" in a blazing tag.

If I knew her name I could look
her up, John, leave a message
after the tone. Take me out.

We could order coffee, hold
court on Charles St. Maybe
she's only in the book

after all. We could visit
the temple, wander inside
its bland stucco walls

smell all the incense
leave our shoes
on the lip of their doors.

■ ■ ■

After the nosey habit-
at of his personal
ad was planted among the other

blue boxes
she didn't once page or pay
for it. Not even a lousy "I Saw You"

after he cruised Charles
made himself a fishbowl
of appearances. So the city

asked me please
compose her a note
too dumb to court alone.

```
MAKE A HELLUVA HEAVEN?

Me: fiesty Reubenesque
w/ appetite for cultures
& even realer estate, all that's

hot & bothersome to taste
ex-pat lifestyle, incendiary self-starter
S/D, H/S, enjoys botanical

ruins, under-
ground malls, financial security
systems & self-help

seeks preservation in self-
same, good bad times, possible
long terminal relationshipment.

Me plotting to
sport you in red the city would like
to meet up somewhere down.
```

■ ■ ■

Spring? It happens
too. Red & yellow tulips finger
gut pink blossoms smear

a stranger fire over us. It's not
rebirth, it's not waking up
to a lively new world

order. Strange to many there is no down-
time. Community service
is cool, your Spring being

very eternal. Got no time
for desire in the Fall
but it makes way.

◩ ◩ ◩

Some of the faceless
heroes lollygag by the ocean
placid in flip-flops

turn themselves over
to the turning heavens
on a spit of sand.

Nobody swims in English Bay
or up the mystery of False Creek.
They ask little

of its nature
other than to seem
perfect.

Typically by day
night (no
decree divides darkness

or light)
they hive in towers
pass piston-quick

through the echoing halls.
Soft electric lamps
they never burn up

above. Today there is sun
rumoured the first hope
for revolution in the weather.

So they gather, bring silver radios
& their cells to the warm sand
by the murky waves, play

up & down their image
& dig the transmissions
from wherever.

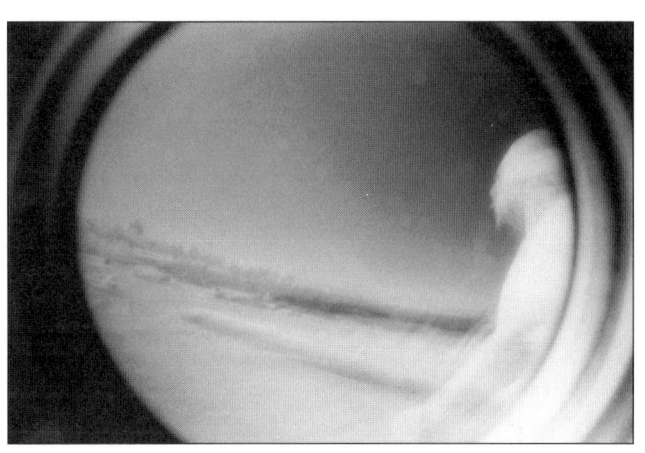

◼ ◼ ◼

In the heart of this plot, John
once there was a zoo. When I was younger
we swarmed on Saturdays.

There was an old man, I remember.
He looked like you. If you were good
& a little mischievous, daring

as this place, he would place
a nut on your head. Squirrels
from the treetop wilds

would steal up your arm & away
with your nut. Terrified us
& loved him for it. Thought

he was other-wise, was magic
touched in the head. But you can hear
the cages are empty now.

Driven mad or diseased
there was a great white bear
leapt years from left

to right, never chased
beyond the frozen flow
of that privacy.

Can you remember, John
what great abstractions
convinced ourselves

the government of this place?
It's crazy what visited you.
It's crazy to think these cages

stand long after the animals
they named. We were young once
kept heroically here

from what? As if the animals
wandered outside the gates
of Chaos.

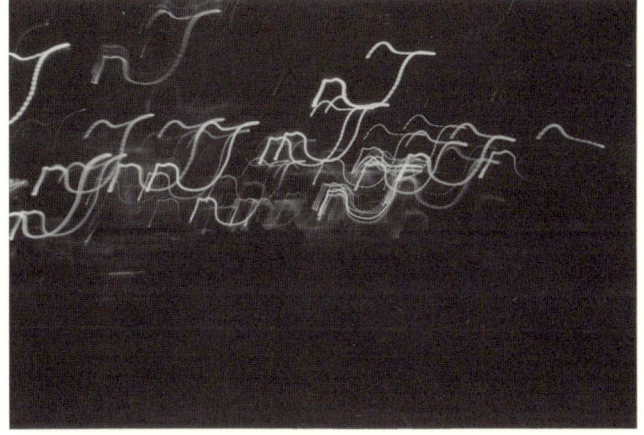

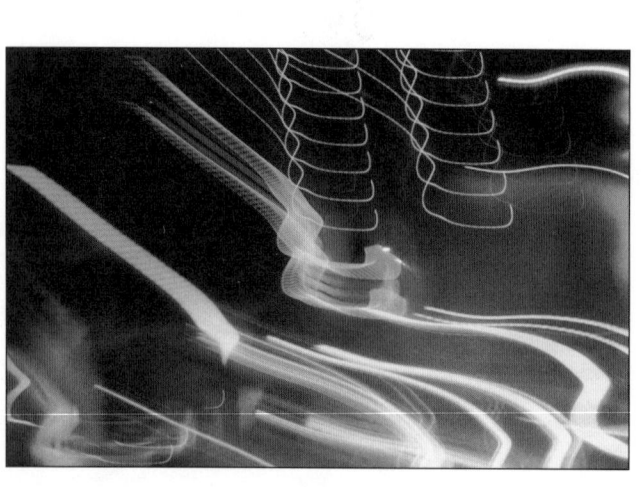

■ ■ ■

The blue TV
lights out picture windows
& into the street

with you
all on TV
going down slow.

Howlin' Wolf the old man's pick
of the war days when he fastened chain-
link for tomatoes to climb.

It's stronger this way
dwelling next to you
all on TV

in the shade
of living
rooms. Hot out-

side blues on the fire
escape. Watch the
engines back up

to the hall & the thrill
go. Stiff the old man up-
stairs cruises News-

world, keeps in
touch with me
this way, some-

times drives down-
town in a red pick-up
a load of

scrap for some
easy cash & easier
time. I saw you

in half-view drive
through the back-
drop of a breaking story.

The reporter says it's a human
interest thing. A young woman
smacked by a delivery

van at the corner
of First & something, off the street
& through the window with you all

on TV she is brought to you by Tide
was a home-care worker in a complex.
A few will miss her

dearly on TV. There's the old man
in his cab cutting through the story
in the back-

ground, a fragment of
one arm steering the other
over the shoulder of a girl

he's got interest in. Coaxed
her from the corner, later
says to me on the escape

there's coaching in the signal
in a look are prices for this & for that
the whole works.

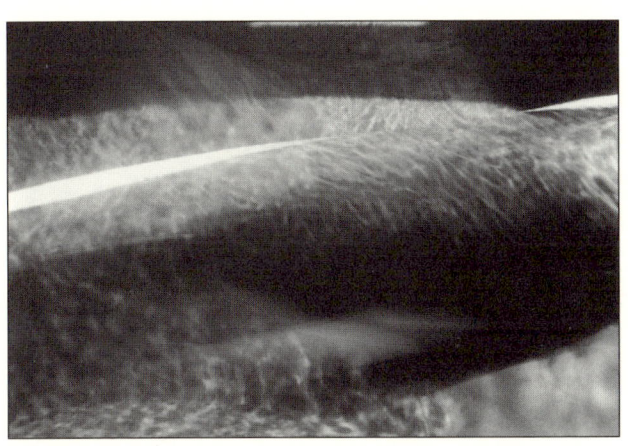

■ ■ ■

Before he backed
into his plot
to the writing & the like

together we tapped
the aquarium glass
as if to us we could call the fish

something intelligent. We tapped
white canes from tank
to tank, more dumb

fish here, & more dumb fish, at least
that's what's imagined.
Could be the message boards.

I sat down by the waters with John.
I wanted to show him the big city
sight. It was unusually cool

beside the waters with John
where a killer whale performs
for little fish. Hundreds of us

we heard there. We sat
down by the waters
to be wetted

to be corralled close to a killer
whale. It leapt & crashed, waved &
splashed in a tedious routine.

'Is that all?' he asked
'This is all there is
to witness?' It is not

a great poem, it is not
worth meeting the city
we are in. There's a tank

& a captive
audience to exhibit the nature
of competitive prices.

■ ■ ■

Back on the bleached
bone of Charles
St. John gone to his own

us would-be *flanneurs* wait for
oblivion in its pleasing shape
of love, our common

emergency. The beaches are full
the towers alive & stoic
with exchange, the beast

scheduled for a 4:00 turn.
I know I have fallen
into a deep & ancient

sleep. The stores are fat
& burning someone
else's dream

something about commandment
& the colours of added value
to this earth

plot by plot. But how
do you go on
to make this place

out of this place? How dare
I see her today, John, glimpsed
on the balls of her feet

cruising the stretch of Grandview
Park. What I saw
& couldn't was that grace-

ful body of
nobody concealed in a stranger
fashion

of red velvet pants. To you
& me & the brightest lures
that hang us up

down here, she is
oblivious
as beauty seems

sometimes best
seems served
blindly.

COLOUR THEORY

Magic, verbal coercion, establishment or management by decree, says, in effect, 'Let there be'—and there was.
—Kenneth Burke

Emergency Broadcast System

Don't ask what compels
to want another poem

other than poetry
is useless

funny unless given to
its curious innovation of time

& spaces given
to warn the long-gone

driver of that ugly Ford
pick-up over there

hey I'm telling you
the lights are on.

Mr. Universe, the First

No matter at first
but for the very big

bang & slow burn of being.
Then God fizzled out after the first week

of membership benefits & New Year's resolution.
What about the love

handles & spankin' new athletic shoes?
Now Sisyphus works

the brilliant machines with savoir-faire
"gimme five more" & "gimme five more".

We set time to the industrial back-
beat of Sis's cool quantum fury

gettin' physical.
We must be for pushing

masses around & tugging
God by his iron ponytail. We say, "come on back

& bench with the best of us
pretty boy." Sissy peacocks

on the dumbbell bench.
Enough to be lifted by

his labour, the numerous pounds
of earthly ignition

in those classical forearms.

A Comfort of Metaphors:
Summer Reading

A moth is not its name
but panic, the gasp of wings
hyperventilating
about the reading lamp.

Panic is an arrow shot
by a glance at a moth
that is not its name, but yours,
for your own reference.

Having lighted, wings smell
of burning flesh, perhaps,
but not yours, not flesh,
but once a moth
of the comfortable air.

The room fills, its odour,
your room, your lover's,
bigger than walls.

Forever in your armchair
cling to a beautiful novel,
the window thrown
open to evening air,
the horrible music of neighbours.

The Ballad of Echolocation

Lighthouse the slick line
a spearing the far sky
for catching the capsize
a shipment of import.

The ocean a body
of mine is the tiding
to slacken the water
the mouth is a coastline.

The old beach a comber
of fingers the trawling
the chancing a gathering
of flesh cut the mooring.

Lighthouse the slick line
a spearing the far sky
for catching the capsize
a shipment of import.

The labour an anchor
of water the secret
the definite nation
a buoy on the last day.

The gutting a chumslop
of fish the alarming
a notion the skullcap
of ocean the longing.

Lighthouse the slick line
a spearing the far sky
for catching the capsize
a shipment of import.

The deep is the hollow
of shell pitched the captain
the whistling a not there
mayday in the once ear.

Blues for Dashboard Mary

Ready Dashboard Mary on a nicotine fuse
blasin' Jeremiah 8-track bullfrog blues
earned a Sally Jesse jaundice for my fidelity runs
lost a trailor park pad soakin' Kingdom Come

Been punchdrunk lonesome on assembly line drift
diggin' punchclock dirt for the graveyard shifts
packin' perfume bombs for your bathtub blessings
so's bridegroom gumshoes smell a way to the
        wedding

But Lady Luck jacked the trailor & she drove her-
        self north
bad luck be a lady boostin' all that I'm worth
she's from ground zero get go spittin' diamonds &
        toads
now the only thing between us is that
        Wonderbread Road

Down Wonderbread Road
that's where Lady Luck stole
no I ain't got a chance with her
& can't find my way home
I'm scratchin' eight
ballin' down Wonderbread Road

Waited Coquihalla long in the dumptruck hours
wantin' cul-de-sac hangtime picket fence flowers
plantin' red mojo roosters in the yellowing grasses
they grew flamingo jingles & her U-turn passes

Once a jitterbug bozo in a back seat rodeo
lazy-boy lovin' the recliners goin' down slow
but that's Xerox powder tarrin' Where You At
        Lane
just a thumb leafin' filthy through its coupon
        book days

Lady Luck she jacked the trailor & she drove her-
    self north
bad luck is a lady boosted all that I'm worth
she's from ground zero get go spittin' diamonds &
    toads
now the only love between us is that
    Wonderbread Road

Down Wonderbread Road
that's where I'll go
I once had a chance
but crapped out on my throw
my luck she pulled up stakes
for that Wonderbread Road

Now I'm Chevy Nova fueled chompin' gear tooth
    ready
gonna bust that hog wild goin' yellow line steady
not a fastfood possum playin' chickenshit soul
but a Leadbelly foot floorin' Midas touch gold

Down Wonderbread Road
just you watch me go
all bets are off
I gotta win place or show
I'm gonna pass Lady Luck by
on that Wonderbread Road

gonna pass Lady Luck up
for that Wonderbread Road

Henri Bergson Gone Done

This white noise of
milk spreads freely
through the coffee
bar.

(11:23, Napoli Café.)

Considers where
happens to be. Once read
"white becomes you"
in a fortune cookie.

(11:23, still.)

Bitter tasting durations.
Breath disperses a fog
of west coast cold shoulder
airs. Sighs
get lost.

(11:24, finally.)

Don't start with me
he threatens her first.
The waitress arrived later.

'11:25, closing in five,' she sings.

Standing drops open
cane. White plastic lengths
extend snap snap snapping.
Presto senses direction.

(11:27.)

Outside listens
inside behind. Considers
when happens
all at once
if only.

VISA
for Robert Sherrin

Five smiling tourists beam
cheery before the Gastown steam-
clock. I do my hospitable best to pass out
of their frame.
Here I am

in a beery afternoon
in the Characters back room
for repartée with Bob. It is raining something awful
on the other side of town.

When they're home from holidays
pictures develop
for family & friends, their five familiar
faces that grinned & patiently
grinned some more waiting wet for the clock
to go off. Meanwhile . . .

Bob & I shoot the breeze in the smoke
about scripts, how he scanned *Chinatown*
for the punchlines. I like that, clean
my glasses & yabber on about six smiling—wait, no
I didn't.

Antipoetry, Animorph

Lower into boiling tub, open cold lips, the glass brim toasts
against his teeth, tastes oak slats of aged port sounds.

He would be okay to abandon ship, poetry's gotta beer gut
life preserver & displaces the scrubbing bubbles displacement.

So many dirty words on the desk, in the real life
marking pile mindset lifestyle.
Two chummy Victoria poets on the radio inside
little ears going under

advice.
(That's not nice.)

It's so nice
to see you, the dancer opened arms & pat-patted
his back
with interruption. "Cut" on someone's documentary
& they all waited out the rain.

She admired the movement
in his new tattoo, the shaky
embrace of two
figures, knot much more than figure there
in the water,
one lithe lizard sticks out a curious neck.

"Careful" cuts
Tracy's voice. Painting two old stools,
"careful not
to get the ink wet yet, babe."

Teenage Preludes
for Jason Le Heup

Long-haired boys on BMX bikes
in a vacant lot

behind any KFC. Spooky old Colonel smiles
down on them, benevolent & grand-

fatherly in his twilight, as if declaring
don't worry about your vegetables

boys, skin is the real
treat. Greasy they slip from the texture

of the world to pop
their wheelies, flip & twirl radical bodies

of chrome, extend themselves
from pedals & grips

into somethin' else. They say it's wicked,
it's awesome. They say it's choice.

Descartes would have slowed
& parked in the drive-thru light, perhaps unreasonably

wept in a practical car
to find philosophy so fast.

With the lighting of the street
lamps, long-haired boys on BMX bikes

take off, astonishing
flash of Camelot, down their avenues

vaulting meridians, leaping from
the old town gridlock. There is no formula

no secret ingredient to cloak
& dagger. They chase down wind

for their hair, for its enduring brand
of estranged mentorship.

When the Yard Sale Bought It

welcome to my hydro box yard sale have everything you could want & already got got erotic grass skirt lampshade diesel powered Weed Whacker look at that ain't she a bute? nuclear resistant baby monitor small ergonomically engineered Indonesian boys 4 for a buck take that to the bank go post-Cold War boom boom 7th floor moustache mortgaged to Kingdome Come & they say the smokin' will get me ceramic mushroom ashtray mantra they keep me in the dark & feed me bullshit no shit read it in Concrete Salvation Digest 4 for a buck & maybe throw in this here cordless Prince Charles screwdriver screw your children down they love it or how 'bout a can of cyanide that's some eatin' kill the little mall rats when you see 'em that's what wisdom in a T-shirt told me hasn't steered me wrong yet sprinkle generously compliments Nintendo buttons & better do it before the Big One gets 'em for you or worse they'll *reproduce* like roaches you got roaches? everyone says you do we had 'em new & improved how 'bout exchanging insurance information? you got a commercial leaf-blower license yet? everyone else has come for a quick-soon bring the wife & mistress & touch base make some of those low fat mutton bars you got from the hamper drive last time we painted the street grey gotta beat that recipe out of you before next Sunday's PTA meeting on Moral Action Against Little League Noise Bylaw Infractions During *Jeopardy* Hours hours of fun for the kids 4 for a buck these designer Hollywood celebrity Pit Bull hybrids are just misunderstood add three cups of water & stir high in fibre domestic as hell after *Hooked On Phonics* & just think of the laughs you'll have how's the Psychic Weather Network business treating you these days? things looking

up for this year's calypso apocalypso? 4 bangs for
your buck would you care to wager an elderly in-
law on it only kidding love old people as often as
possible interested in an antique telephone pole
tube of pornography 1974 UFO operator's manu-
al lots of valuable real estate artifacts act now
stuff's goin' fast before City Council pulls the plug
on my life support already removed the bionic
remote for the family satellite & next thing you
know our fine little Community Watch spies
what's in the trash & passes a motion to shoot my
husband wife & kids

Method (ii)

We're in clean with the landlord.
He invites us in French.
The stairwell is blue.

The stairwell is not blue.
Eh-ven bleu if you plees.
I've one eye left.

I've one glass eye he watches.
The iris is blue.
Its ghost swings in the hollow.

The iris is ghost blue or maybe heaven.
There is a chip in his floorboards.
Our shoes are fine he assures.

How to ask can we live here.
The carpets will save us from the dead.
They gather in our old digs and jump.

We've suffered their barefeet and a lease.
The hardwood is always dusty always dusty.
Glass eyes roll on slanting floors it's true.

Always their want to make noise the dead.
The landlord nods his understanding up and down.
There's French inside it and blue.

Tracy can see it now.
She says you would work there.
Most things compose in the window.

A picture window is like comparison.
Always the want to write that there.
It proposes its little beyond plain.

Five Deep Cove Stanzas

A frail cottage
of many rooms, precarious
on the edge

of a dark forest
& a deep lake.
Precious retreat

slopes from the imagination
where dozers cleared a small plot
for bony hands

to erect the rest
that is not the rest
inside. Between us welcome

a darker forest
a deeper lake
here to summer in.

What Leaves Us: Seasonal Hymn

Step naturally into this
contortionist's rain.
The initial sign of coming
Fall & beloved resignation.

All the garish tops
are freaking out
as we shift hokey-pokey
our drippy postures
the fleshless expressions
we carry on.

September leaves me forever
clueless. Absently stole all this
way before only to turn
& the sky applauds your antics
with ransom notes.

Step freely from the safe
sidewalk show & plunge into the usual
traffic. We are owed this
hostile impatience.

The electric hand across Graveley
is signing off, so far off
it can't be my own
manipulations to hang on
       for your life
just hang on there a sec.

On About

The most best part of morning
erroneously pissed away
marking the English

diagnostic tests. Language
an illness till the end
I guest. As for a boy

a topic, a tropic
sentence fragment I
scribbled I wuz here
warm in a drift of snow

you wouldn't find no more.
Whimsy released its swivel
first from young hips.

But first I would like to argue with the advantages
that come
with advancing sex. & in conclusion it will be
very redundantly clear
to the reader there's a huge big difference growing
between sex & harassment.

Irregardless those floodplains
they don't freeze no more
winter having fucked
off for the most best part.

It's currently spent sweating about unhealthy
relations with my ThinkPad
fingers & palms clammy, excited
with the dribble of current
upright in arm hairs.

But still won't run from those magnetic
drifts, a boy's tongue

stuck to the CP tracks
gumboots hitched to the thin
muscle of magnetic fields

of language. They encourage the young
with tumours. Be encouraged
when I say begin to please

press the point
of your thesis or pen or

click & drag
out what ails you. Language
the vast & ugly relief
taken there to revisit.

Gluttony

The refrigerator belongs
to so many poems
on it, I've devoured
them all, at least once

stored my own
preserves there, whatever
feast or famine.

Fresh, you can't help suffering
melodramatic airs. The fridge
mesmerized your mother

cradled your first efforts
with magnetic letters.
Early kitchen life is dark

& chilling, the midnight
icebox, its relentless chatter. Open up
force a minor blast.

What the hell are you looking for?
Difficult to stomach it's empty
save that flickering bulb
of our open close open door philosophies.

Cutting the National Tracks: A Purdy

1. HORSE POWER

One hand reining
jeeps and fords and chevvys
over roads devising man's
screaming highlands.
Were thunder hooves.

2. IMPERMANENT

Maddening, I couldn't find
all the different parts of me
      the sunlit reefs
an unending account
in a postcard back to you about my faithfulness.
Anxious and uneasy I glimpse
never being intended.

3. TRANS

hear the rumbling iron singing
mile after dusty mile

thru dockyard streets and dingy dowager houses
puddles on Water Street

move east away from the sunset
the mapmaker's belly

right behind you
the boxcar doorway

4. GRAVE NATION

A footnote on human character:

a dead old woman
Montreal
in our conversation.

In the manner of friends
I walk among the down
the sun stretching.

From head to headland
a blackness
like growing swans.

Most improbable.

5. SUN AND MOON

Lying together
a heart boils
white.

6. DETAIL

It bears fruit every year.
Small bitter apples.

They were there and that's all.
The tree, leafless.

7. INTERRUPTION

Look out
together

for 20 minutes every night
over the leftovers.

8. ARTIFACT

Carved ivory swans
with their long ships

in a cycle.
Heads

for six hundred years
nearly

out of his mind
where pictures are.

History begins to cover him
the ivory thought.

9. RUN

The rain does not come.
I am hungry for home
ground. Us half ghosts.

But there are fish here
past land
beyond trees.

10. GANGS OF KOSMOS

They stand upright
pride in being

pale, close to what they truly are:
a god's indulgence

because he pitied men
they said.

Land beings together
the secret still

instead of going forward to the planets
topple.

NOTE: In a manner of speaking, this sequence was found in *15x2 Canadian Poets* (Gary Geddes, ed). Each poem here takes its vocabulary & line from every second and fifteenth line of those anthologized Purdy verses. Curiously, of all those poets, Purdy's compositions lent themselves most generously.

Graven Image Tag

You know, *Tetris*. That's what it's called, *Tetris*. You know, it's like—

Ya, ya, *Tetris*, I know. I totally love it too, right, well, at least I used to when it first came out. But now it's not so, you know, good or in'eresting 'cause it's just all the same all the time with the pieces falling—

Oh, I totally play it all the time. When I'm at work and the mall's dead, or we're just cashing out, I'll be like playing it on my graphic calculator pronto. Or at school when the prof or whatever is, you know, is talking about the lecture, and I feel like zoning, I'll play then too. I just can't stop, right? I mean, I just can't stop. I like play it with the sound off, you know, on top of my book when I have it open, kind of under the table like as if I'm reading or somethin'—

Ya, and what do you graph on those things anyway?

I dunno yet.

Ya, that's pretty cool but *Dracula*'s way better, like *way* much more. It's got that awesome music that goes kinda *da dada duh da da dada duh*, you know what I mean? I used to play *Solitaire* before that. I'd play even before I'd get in the shower in the morning and my mom, she used to worry and say, like she'd go, you spend way too much time doing that stuff, way too much—

Ya the music's okay but I like the math part. Like, *Tetris is* math and like you have to think in shapes and stuff like that. I do that all the time, right? Like after I play a long time or something, I'll be like all lookin' around or driving or whatever and think how everything fits like, you know, *together* and it really freaks me out sometimes and I think whoa—

Ya. I've got this friend who—

But you know what I mean, right? It's like you're sittin' there across from me and your legs and back and stuff like that fit totally perfectly into the seat, and so does everyone on the bus—

Ya, I've got this friend Duncan, only we call him Drunken 'cause he's like that, and, anyways, he says—

But I mean we can move and then our feet fit totally on the floor and like your hands, they fit when you pull the buzzer cord thing and stuff like that. It's so creepy in a way and sometimes I think that's like what makes us want—

Ya, it's like my dad works nights, right? doin' construction stuff, but not houses or nothin' like that. He's one of those guys who works on the roads at night, right? 'cause there's less traffic and people and stuff. Only, this one time, a kid I know from school got soooo pissed at my dad for making him wait there that the kid gunned his van at my dad and tried to run him over. I mean, he isn't even the guy or person or whatever who holds the stop sign. But, oh ya, it's like I remember when I was young, say seven or something, I realized that if I'm standing in the driveway or somewhere like that, it's connected to anywhere and so, in a way, I'm always touching everywhere at once too, like, I dunno, Ottawa and L.A. Places like that—

But not Victoria, right? or some other continent, right?

Ya, I guess not, but, ya, I am if you think of the ferry as a kind of water road, right? Well, you know what I mean—

Ya. It's kinda like what my prof was saying about Freud 'cause Freud said when you're born it's like an ocean or, you know, everything is just you. You think like that anyways, and so the prof, he says that you always wanna be like that or get back to being that way with yourself and that's why people believe in God or whatever. You know, stuff like that. Do you ever do that thing where you think, like, what's a dog and you kinda say it over and over in your head. Dog   dog   dog   dog. And then it's like it doesn't mean anything anymore or nothin'—

Ya, like my mom showed me a book from when she was in school a long time ago and there was this thing in there about Freud, 'cause I had to do that paper, right? and it said how he was doing all these interviews or experiments or whatever with girls or something and then he found out there was a lot of, you know, incest going on in the olden days with their dads and brothers and stuff, but it just didn't go with what he thought so he just ignored it all—

Ya, like they do that, right? They say, well, I guess this doesn't matter so much, no big deal—

Ya, *exactly*. He's all, like, oh well, I just won't talk about this thing which matters a lot. I mean, so why do we need to read him anyways if he wasn't even, you know, accurate—

Ya, totally. But then I guess later he musta changed his mind when he said that gross thing about how like everyone wants to do their mothers and fathers and that kinda stuff . . .

THE WICKEDNESS THAT SLEEPS IN STONE

A prospect
of hapless stones
before my feet.

This one
& this one   I can't
say what about
          more.

Don't know much about
temporary things.
Can't say as I do

as I do.
All I want to know is
what time you got, kid?

The neighbour's boy is taken

          (white blond shock
          of his hair)

with making himself
a mountain

of little rocks.
Making himself the landing.

What a wonderful world this
this would-be.

From his swing set
he is slingshot
from the laws all
barefoot & slaphappy
as the chosen sun.

I only want to say this.

In his soles
sure he felt that

impressive giving away.

Mountain.

Standard time.

'BROTHER OF DEATH AND
FORGETTING...'

hypno
tic early rit
ual siren us
ually with al
arm arm clock
ed snooze on
ce more again
st better get
up judge
ment

twin bed fell
ow under dis
covery blank
et air blue ceil
ing again
st what so
called cold sea
son drea
mer of wilder
ness waters

water strip
ping pong of
fence of drop
lets suit
able soap skin
ned under
world bath
tub boat
man to
ken

clothes line
d close
t says gree

n black n yell
ow what old col
lour lured him al
ive all
ive oh

diner break
fast no
thing bet
ter than a toas
t coffee n saus
age can come be
fore from he
re on in to
day

Colour Theory
for Rory Knighton

Look, Tracy says, it works this way. Green
is to disappear all the others. What I didn't know

when a throaty peel of "Twist and Shout"
burns through the joint.

Two Ringos two tables away, gassed & uptempo
for a decade they heard

about, want custody of the myth
called good time.

My ales vanish without a clue.
She says you'll find green is not printed

but you can see it
there in not being the other colours.

But that green
on TV is different, illuminated & projected

to you, in you, as its
self? Now the pool table is crawling in

my eye rolling trajectories back to him
self? My brother is a blond child

in his Mr. Turtle pool.
There is no water

& no way. But I am
there like the water that is not

there when he weeps for it to fill the empty
belly of his creature, for himself

to fill some future. So I turn
that world on its back, switch

channels above the bar.
I am turning on the old green hose for you.

Water in its elastic shape
of memory is workin' on out

the throat of a coiled & sleeping snake. I
know it is poison

to kill off a dying past
to spring some new present to life, but for you

with love I am shaking & drowning that flicker
you are you are not.

ACKNOWLEDGMENTS:

The author would like to extend his gratitudes to the following friends & readers: George Bowering, Thea Bowering, Mark Cochrane, Wayde Compton, Brad Cran, Brian Fawcett, Reg Johanson, Brian Kaufman, Jason Le Heup, Tracy Rawa, George Stanley, Anne Stone, Sharon Thesen, Christina Turnbull, Michael Turner & Karina Vernon.

Special thanks to Robert Sherrin for the photography collaboration & Vancouver walks which helped compose "From Charles Street, Pandemonium."

Earlier & often sketchier versions of some poems have appeared in the following publications: *The Capilano Review, Descant, Fiddlehead, The Malahat Review, Prairie Fire, PRISM International, Rampike, sub-TERRAIN* & *Hammer & Tongs: A Smoking Lung Anthology.*

A number of poems from "What Leaves Us" appear in a chapbook under that title (Smoking Lung Press). Two alternate media versions of "Graven Image Tag" appear in a pulley press chapbook. This piece also appeared as an installation/reading at Presentation House Gallery (North Vancouver) and Artspeak Gallery (Vancovuer).

 Ryan Knighton was born in Langley, B.C., in the formative 1970s. His poetry and prose have appeared in numerous Canadian journals & magazines. A member of the English Department at Capilano College, he teaches literature & other writings & currently serves as editor of *The Capilano Review*. In East Vancouver, where he makes his home, passers-by often find his blindness worthy of comment, praise or scrutiny.